A Tower
Stands Tall

Kylie Burns
Crabtree Publishing Company
www.crabtreebooks.com

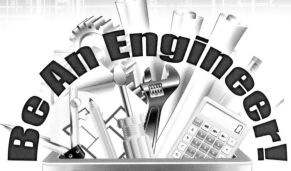

Be An Engineer!
Designing to Solve Problems

Author: Kylie Burns

Series research and development:
Janine Deschenes and Reagan Miller

Editorial director: Kathy Middleton

Editor: Petrice Custance

Proofreader: Kathy Middleton

Design and photo research: Katherine Berti

Print and production coordinator: Katherine Berti

Images:

Alamy Stock Photo
ITAR-TASS News Agency: p. 22

Dreamstime
Erinpackardphotography: p. 5

Shutterstock
kaprik: p. 17 center
V. Ben: p. 7 right

All other images by Shutterstock

Thank you to Crystal and John Sikkens for their valuable input.

Library and Archives Canada Cataloguing in Publication

Burns, Kylie, author
     A tower stands tall / Kylie Burns.

(Be an engineer! Designing to solve problems)
Includes index.
Issued in print and electronic formats.
ISBN 978-0-7787-5162-5 (hardcover).--
ISBN 978-0-7787-5166-3 (softcover).--
ISBN 978-1-4271-2110-3 (HTML)

     1. Towers--Design and construction--Juvenile literature.
2. Towers--Juvenile literature. 3. Structural engineering--Juvenile
literature. I. Title.

TA660.T6B86 2018   j690'.597   C2018-902997-8
                                                                C2018-902998-6

Library of Congress Cataloging-in-Publication Data

Names: Burns, Kylie, author.
Title: A tower stands tall / Kylie Burns.
Description: New York, New York : Crabtree Publishing Company,
     [2019] | Series: Be an engineer! Designing to solve problems |
     Includes index.
Identifiers: LCCN 2018027894 (print) | LCCN 2018029210 (ebook) |
     ISBN 9781427121103 (Electronic) |
     ISBN 9780778751625 (hardcover) |
     ISBN 9780778751663 (paperback)
Subjects: LCSH: Towers--Design and construction--Juvenile literature.
Classification: LCC TH2180 (ebook) | LCC TH2180 .B87 2019 (print) |
     DDC 725/.97--dc23
LC record available at https://lccn.loc.gov/2018027894

Crabtree Publishing Company

www.crabtreebooks.com   1-800-387-7650

Printed in the U.S.A./092018/CG20180719

Published in Canada
Crabtree Publishing
616 Welland Ave.
St. Catharines, Ontario
L2M 5V6

Published in the United States
Crabtree Publishing
PMB 59051
350 Fifth Avenue, 59th Floor
New York, New York 10118

Published in the United Kingdom
Crabtree Publishing
Maritime House
Basin Road North, Hove
BN41 1WR

Published in Australia
Crabtree Publishing
3 Charles Street
Coburg North
VIC 3058

Contents

Hi, I'm Ava and this is Finn. Get ready for an inside look at the world of engineering! The Be an Engineer! series explores how engineers build structures to solve problems.

After reading this book, join us online at Crabtree Plus to help us solve real-world engineering challenges! Just use the Digital Code on page 23 in this book.

The Sky's the Limit

Carly is excited to be moving from the busy city to a big farm. One day, her parents plan to grow wheat on the new farm. They have to wait because right now there is nowhere to store the grain after the wheat is **harvested**. As they begin the drive to the new farm, Carly wonders where they might store the grain.

Carly knows their new farm has a barn. She asks her mother if the grain can be stored in the barn. Carly's mother says it cannot be stored there because the barn will be full of machinery and equipment. As they drive away from the city, Carly looks up at the tall buildings from her car window. Suddenly, Carly has a thought. A tower would be perfect for storing grain!

Did you know?

A **silo** is a type of tower. It is used to store materials, such as grain and other food products. Silos can be 30 to 275 feet (9 to 84 m) high.

*A tower is a structure that is taller than it is wide. Some towers are hollow **cylinders** that store things. Others are solid and are used to **support** other things .*

What Is an Engineer?

Carly is thinking like an engineer. An engineer is a person who uses math, science, and creative thinking skills to design things to help solve problems.

All Kinds of Engineers

There are many different kinds of engineers. Designing buildings, roads, spaceships, towers, and even medicines requires engineers with different kinds of knowledge. One engineer might design a tower's shape. Another might create the materials used to build it. Most engineers work as part of a team.

The CN Tower in Toronto, Canada, is wide at the bottom and narrow at the top. It is made of concrete. This shape and material help the tower remain **stable** in strong winds. The tower supports a restaurant and viewing area near the top.

Engineers Solve Problems

Problems aren't always easy to solve. All engineers follow the same steps to solve a problem. This set of steps is called the Engineering Design Process. The steps in this process can be repeated over and over until a safe and **effective** solution is found. Making mistakes is often part of this process.

The Engineering Design Process

1 ASK
Ask questions and gather information about the problem you are trying to solve.

2 BRAINSTORM
Work with a group to come up with different ideas to solve the problem. Choose the best solution.

3 PLAN AND MAKE A MODEL
Create a plan to carry out your solution. Draw a diagram and gather materials. Make a **model** of your solution.

4 TEST AND IMPROVE
Test your model and record the results. Using the results, improve, or make your design better. Retest your improved design.

5 COMMUNICATE
Share your design with others.

Asking Questions

Engineers ask questions in order to gather information about the problem they need to solve. This is the first step in the Engineering Design Process. If an engineer needs to build a tower that will help farmers store grain, it is important to find out what the **environment** is like in the area. Things such as wind, weather patterns, and population can affect the environment where a tower may be built.

Asking questions and researching the answers helps an engineer to find the best solution to a problem.

PEOPLE PER
SQUARE MILE

2,000.0 to 69,468.4
500.0 to 1,999.9
88.4 to 499.9
20.0 to 88.3
1.0 to 19.9
0.0 to 0.9

Brainstorming

Once engineers have gathered their information, they brainstorm, or discuss possible solutions with others. An engineer may use a diagram like this one to keep track of ideas while brainstorming.

Problem

There is nowhere to store grain on the farm once it is harvested

Remove equipment from the barn to make room to store the grain.

Build a tower, such as a silo, designed for storing grain.

Take it to another farm for storage.

Put the grain in many large, sealed containers.

Planning

If the team decides a silo is the best solution, engineers will make the plan to build it. They first need to consider the surrounding environment when choosing where to put the silo. Then, they need to choose building materials that will help keep the grain cool and dry. The silo design must keep water and animals out. Engineers often choose concrete or steel for building silos.

Did you know?

A group of silos is called a grain elevator. This is because an elevator system is used to move the grain. Buckets scoop up the grain and move it to the top of the storage silos.

This grain elevator has several tower silos made from concrete.

Solid towers are often wider at the bottom. This creates a strong structure that won't fall over in wind or storms. Towers are built to stand without support from cables attached to the ground. They are not the same as skyscrapers because they are not designed to be homes or offices for people.

Wind turbines are tall towers with large blades attached. The blades must be high above the ground so they can catch the wind. The blades spin, which creates electricity.

The Tokyo Skytree tower in Japan is the tallest tower in the world. It is 2,080 feet (634 m) tall. Engineers built it with **reinforced concrete** *to make it strong enough to withstand earthquakes.*

Creating a Model

Once the planning stage is complete, engineers create a model of the tower. A model is a **representation** of a real object. A model allows engineers to test and improve their design. Engineers use the model to explain their design to others.

*A model can be made as a **3-D** object or as a drawing using a computer program. This 3-D printer is making a model from plastic.*

Testing and Improving

A model is used to test the design of a tower. Forces such as wind or extreme temperatures can be created so the model tower can be tested against them. These tests help engineers learn if the tower will be stable enough to withstand any kind of weather. After each test, engineers record the results and make improvements to the model. They perform the tests many times in order to be sure the design is safe.

Did you know?

Every tall tower **sways** in the wind. A wind tunnel can create the force of high-speed wind to test how much a tower model will sway. If engineers find the tower sways too much, they make changes to the design and test it again.

Sharing the Results

The last step in the Engineering Design Process is for engineers to share their results. This helps engineers determine which designs work, and which do not. They share results to make sure towers are built safely. Over time, sharing results has improved the design and the stability of towers around the world.

Eiffel Tower

Engineers learn from each other. In 1889, the Eiffel Tower was built in Paris, France. It was the world's tallest structure. At the time, its design and the use of iron as a building material were unusual. Iron is light, but very strong. Since then, engineers have used the same kind of design to build towers, like this one that carries electricity.

Then and Now

Early towers were built for many purposes. The view from a watchtower made it possible to see enemies from far away. A church bell in a tower could be heard ringing throughout the town. A light at the top of a lighthouse could be seen by ships at sea. Today, we use towers to support **communication** equipment, hold up cables that carry electricity, store crops, and as tourist attractions.

Early towers were built with materials such as wood, stone, or iron. Today, engineers often use a combination of materials, such as steel frames, reinforced concrete, and glass.

bell tower

watchtower

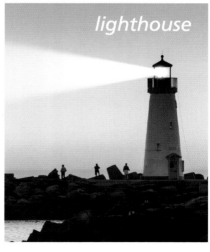

lighthouse

Step by Step

Safety and stability are very important when designing a tower. Engineers must follow each step in the Engineering Design Process closely. If they do not, they may make a mistake in the design of the tower that causes a serious problem. Following each of the steps in this process can help prevent a disaster.

Tower Trouble

In 1178, a tower being built in Pisa, Italy, started to sink under the weight of the structure. Known today as the Leaning Tower of Pisa, the structure leans more than 16 feet (5 m) to one side! If the engineers had first tested a model, they would have discovered the sandy soil underneath was not strong enough to support the tower's weight.

Today, teams of engineers do research and share their results before building a tower. Once the tower is built, engineers must check it regularly for any weak or damaged areas so they can be fixed right away.

Model Activity

Using a model to test a tower design is an important step in the Engineering Design Process. It allows engineers to discover how forces such as shape, weight, wind, and weather patterns might affect the tower's safety and stability. Try building your own model of a tower, and test its ability to stand tall and stable.

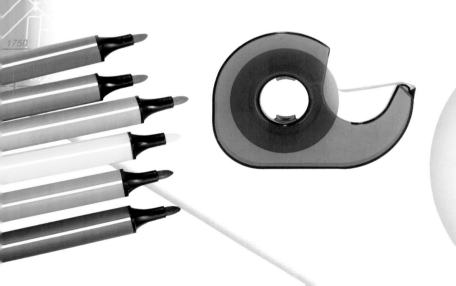

You will need:

3 letter-sized sheets of cardstock

tape

marker

several small books of the same size and weight

Instructions:

The goal is to discover a stable tower shape that can remain standing under the weight of several books.

1. With one sheet of cardstock, make two folds to create a triangular prism shape (see right). Seal the open side with tape.
2. Stand your tower on a flat surface and place one book at a time on top. How many books does it hold before the tower buckles? Record your results.
3. With a second sheet of cardstock, make three folds to make a rectangular prism shape (see right). Seal the open side with tape. Repeat Step 2.
4. Roll the final sheet of cardstock into the shape of a cylinder (see right). Seal the open side with tape. Repeat Step 2.

What did you observe?

Which tower shape held the most books before buckling?

Which shape of tower would you choose if you were building a real tower?

Avoiding Disaster

The Ostankino Tower in Moscow, Russia, was the first tower to reach a height of 1,640 feet (500 m). On August 27, 2000, a fire broke out inside the tower. Over 300 firefighters had to carry equipment up the tower to fight the fire. Although the fire destroyed the inside of the tower, the outer structure was not damaged.

The Ostankino Tower is a communications tower built with concrete, steel, and glass. The main structure didn't collapse because the engineers built a solid tower out of stable material.

Learning More

Books

Engineering Close-up series. Crabtree Publishing Company, 2014.

Beck, Barbara. *The Future Architect's Handbook*. Schiffer Publishing, 2014.

Dillon, Patrick. *The Story of Buildings: From the Pyramids to the Sydney Opera House and Beyond*. Candlewick, 2014.

For fun engineering challenges, activities, and more, enter the code at the Crabtree Plus website below.

www.crabtreeplus.com/be-an-engineer

Your code is:
bae04

Websites

http://tryengineering.org
Check out this site for fun quizzes such as, "What Kind of Engineer are You?" and to find engineering game apps for your devices.

http://pbskids.org/zoom/activities/build
Discover interesting facts, and cool science activities such as building towers out of straws, marshmallows, and paper.

https://easyscienceforkids.com/cn-tower-facts/
This site shares interesting facts about the structure of Toronto's CN Tower.

Glossary

Note: Some boldfaced words are defined where they appear in the book.

3-D (THREE-DEE) *adjective*
Short for three-dimensional, an object that has length, width, and height

communication (kuh-myoo-ni-KEY-shuhn) *noun* Connecting and sharing information in a variety of ways

cylinder (SIL-in-der) *noun*
A solid shape with bases on each end that are circles and a curved surface that joins the bases

effective (ih-FEK-tiv) *adjective*
Producing the correct result

environment (en-VAHY-ern-muh-nt) *noun* The surroundings in which a person, plant, or animal lives

harvest (HAHR-vist) *verb*
To gather a crop

model (MOD-l) *noun*
A representation of a real object

reinforced concrete
(ree-in-FOHRSD KON-kreet) *noun*
Concrete that has been made stronger by placing metal rods or bars inside

representation (rep-ri-zen-TEY-shun) *noun* Something that stands in place for something else

silo (SAHY-loh) *noun*
A large storage bin for crops or animal feed, usually found on farms

stable (STEY-buhl) *adjective*
Strong, unable to be moved easily

support (suh-PAWRT) *verb*
To hold up or bear the weight of something

sway (swey) *verb*
Move from side to side

wind turbine (wind TUR-bahyn) *noun*
A tower with blades that converts wind into electricity

A noun is a person, place, or thing.
An adjective is a word that tells you what something is like.
A verb is an action word that tells you what someone or something does.

Index